Editor

Eric Migliaccio

Editor in Chief

Karen J. Goldfluss, M.S. Ed.

Creative Director

Sarah M. Smith

Cover Artist

Barb Lorseyedi

Art Coordinator

Renée Mc Elwee

Illustrator

Clint McKnight

Imaging

James Edward Grace

Publisher

Mary D. Smith, M.S. Ed.

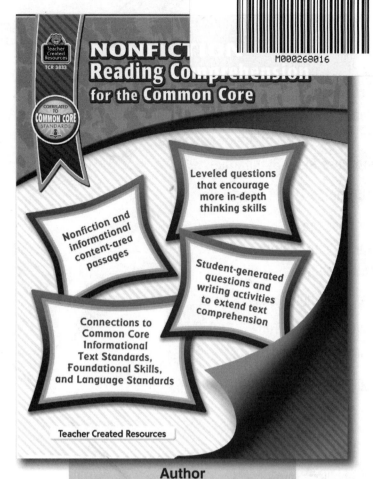

Author

Tracie Heskett, M.Ed.

For correlations to Common Core State Standards, see page 8 of this book or visit *http://www.teachercreated.com/standards/*.

Teacher Created Resources

6421 Industry Way
Westminster, CA 92683
www.teachercreated.com

ISBN: 978-1-4206-3833-2

© 2014 Teacher Created Resources
Made in U.S.A.

Table of Contents

Introduction

Reading and comprehending nonfiction or informational text is a challenge. Not everyone can do it well, and it needs to be specifically taught. Students who are great at reading narratives like *Lord of the Rings* or *The Princess Diaries* may still quiver at the possibility of having to understand instructions on uploading an assignment to DropBox. Students who love reading historical fiction may be fearful of reading history. Students who, with flashlight in hand, hide beneath their sheets reading the end of a science-fiction book may glaze over at the sight of an actual factual science article.

Nevertheless, informational text is all around us, and reading it well just takes working out a certain muscle — an informational-text muscle, if you will.

This book is meant to be an informational-muscle gym. Each activity is meant to build in complexity, and each activity is meant to push students in both their reading and their ability to display what they understand about what they read.

In addition to a practice passage, there are 18 reading selections contained in this book. The selections are separated into units, based on their subject matter. As a result, no matter the content area you teach, you will find applicable selections here on which your students can practice.

It doesn't matter what state you teach in, what grade level you teach, or what subject you teach; this book will aid students in understanding more deeply the difficult task of reading informational and nonfiction texts.

Reading Comprehension and the Common Core

The Common Core Standards are here, and with them come a different way to think about reading comprehension. In the past, reading informational text had been compartmentalized, each piece an isolated activity. The Common Core way of thinking is slightly different.

The goal is for students to read different genres and selections of text, pull them together in their heads, and be able to derive a theme or topic that may be shared by them all. In other words, a student may be given three different texts from three different points of view or three different genre standpoints and then have to think about their own thoughts on the subject.

Perhaps a student looks at the following:

1. Instructions on downloading an image from a digital camera
2. A biography about a famous photographer
3. A Google search history on the invention of the camera from the past to the present

Then, from those pieces, the student must pull a common theme or opinion on the topic.

Introduction *(cont.)*

Reading Comprehension and the Common Core *(cont.)*

But to be able to synthesize text (put the thoughts together), a student must first be able to read individual texts and analyze them (pull them apart). That's where this series of books comes in.

Nonfiction Reading Comprehension for the Common Core helps students to hone in on a specific piece of text, identify what's the most important concept in that piece, and answer questions about that specific selection. This will train your students for the bigger challenge that will come later in their schooling: viewing multiple texts and shaking out the meaning of them all.

If you are a public-school teacher, you may be in a state that has adopted the Common Core Standards. Use the selections in this book as individual reading-comprehension activities or pair them with similarly themed selections from other genres to give students a sense of how they will have to pull understanding from the informational, text-heavy world around us.

Copy the individual worksheets as is; or, if you are looking for a more Common Core-aligned format, mimic the Common Core multiple-choice assessments that are coming our way by entering the questions into websites that can help create computer adaptive tests (CATs).

CATs are assessments that allow a student to answer a question, which, depending on whether they answered it correctly or not, leads them to the next question that may be more geared to his or her level. In other words, each student will be taking a differentiated assessment that will end up indicating if a student is capable of answering "Novice" questions up to "Expert" questions.

There are many websites out there that can help you develop assessments to mimic those planned. Create the quiz and embed it into your class webpage or document:

Here are just a couple:

- *http://www.gotoquiz.com/create.html*
- *http://www.quibblo.com/*

Use the selections from this book, and then enter the corresponding questions into the quiz generators. We have identified questions that are higher or lower in level by assigning them a "weight" (from single-weight up through triple-weight). This weight system provides a glimpse of how hard a student should work in order to answer the question correctly. (For more information, read "Leveled Questions" on page 5.)

Regardless of how you choose to use this book, introducing students to the informational world at large is an important way to help them build skills that they will use throughout their schooling and beyond.

Introduction *(cont.)*

Leveled Questions

As you go through this book, you will notice that each question that students will be answering is labeled with icons that look like weights. These icons represent different levels of difficulty. The levels are based on Costa's Levels of Questioning.

The questions in this book are divided into three levels:

Level 1	Level 2	Level 3

These include sentence stems that ask students to . . .	*These include sentence stems that ask students to . . .*	*These include sentence stems that ask students to . . .*
Recite **Define** **Describe** **List**	**Infer** **Compare/Contrast** **Sequence** **Categorize**	**Judge** **Evaluate** **Create** **Hypothesize** **Predict**

The icons are a visual way to make these levels clear to students. That is important because students need to be able to recognize that some questions may require more effort and thought to answer.

Now, most of the multiple-choice questions in this book happen to fall into the Level 1 and Level 2 categories. That is pretty standard for multiple-choice questions. After all, how can asking to create something be defined by an A, B, C, or D answer? However, we may have found a way around that.

At the end of each worksheet is a place for students to develop their own questions about the material they have just read. This brings in a deeper-thinking opportunity. Having your students ask higher-level questions is a great way for assessing their comprehension of what they have read. The deeper the student's question, the deeper his or her understanding of the material.

A student handout called "The Questioning Rubric" is provided on page 6. It serves two purposes:

- It gives your students concrete examples of the elements that make up the different levels of questions.

- It gives you, the teacher, a way to determine whether a student-generated question is a low- or high-level inquiry.

The goal of a student is to ask more challenging questions of oneself. The goal of the teacher is to be able to track better the level of production for each student. This book helps do both.

Introduction (cont.)

The Questioning Rubric

Answering questions is one way of proving you understand a reading selection. However, creating your very own questions about the selection might be an even better way. Developing thoughtful, high-level questions can really display your understanding of what you have read, and it also makes other students think about the reading passage in a unique way.

So what types of questions can you ask? There are three levels of questions, and for each one there is a different amount of work your brain must do to answer the question. We've chosen to use a symbol of a weight in order to represent this amount. Consult this chart when thinking about what defines a great question as compared to a so-so one.

Icon	Description
	A single weight represents a **Level 1** question that doesn't require much brainpower to answer correctly. The question only asks readers to tell what they know about the selection. For example, any inquiry that asks for a simple "Yes or No" or "True or False" response is a Level 1 question.
	A double weight represents a **Level 2** question that requires you to use a little more brain sweat. (Ewww!) This question asks readers to think a little beyond the passage. It may require some analysis, inference, or interpretation. Questions involving comparing/contrasting or sequencing often fall here.
	A **Level 3** question really makes you work for its answer. These questions allow you to show off your knowledge of a topic by asking you to create, wonder, judge, evaluate, and/or apply what you know to what you think. These types of questions are much more open-ended than Level 1 or Level 2 questions.

Don't be scared to sweat a little in answering or developing Level 3 questions. Working out your brain in this way will help prepare you for some heavy lifting later on in life. So as you progress through this book, use this rubric as a resource to make sure your questions are as high-level as possible.

Need help getting started? The following sentence stems will give you ideas about how to create questions for each level.

Level 1
- Write the definition of…
- Describe how _____ is…
- List the details that go into…

Level 2
- What can you infer from _____?
- Compare _____ with _____.
- Contrast _____ with _____.
- Write the steps in sequence from _____.
- Place _____ in the right category.

Level 3
- How would you judge the _____?
- How would you evaluate the _____?
- How can you create a _____?
- Hypothesize what would happen if _____.
- What do you predict will happen in _____?

Introduction *(cont.)*

Achievement Graph

As you correct your responses in this book, track how well you improve. Calculate how many answers you got right after each worksheet and mark your progress here based on the number of weights each question was worth. For instance, if you get the first problem correct and it is worth two weights, then write "2" in the first column. Do this for each column, and add up your total at the end.

Reading Passage	1	2	3	4	Total
"Racing into History"					
"An Oddly Delicious Fruit"					
"A Thrilling Ride"					
"The Sleep Hormone"					
"The World's Wildest Weather"					
"A Code for Health"					
"Folly or Investment?"					
"War on the Home Front"					
"Our Valuable Money"					
"Vending Machines"					
"The History of Fashion"					
"René Descartes"					
"César Chávez"					
"J.R.R. Tolkien"					
"Admiral Hopper"					
"Ultimate: The Game"					
"The Nobel Prizes"					
"Giving a Great Speech"					
"Designing a Skatepark"					

Common Core State Standards

The lessons and activities included in *Nonfiction Reading Comprehension for the Common Core, Grade 8* meet the following Common Core State Standards. (©Copyright 2010. National Governors Association Center for Best Practices and Council of Chief State School Officers. All rights reserved.) For more information about the Common Core State Standards, go to *http://www.corestandards.org/* or visit *http://www.teachercreated.com/standards/*.

Informational Text Standards	
Craft and Structure	**Pages**
CCSS.ELA.RI.8.4. Determine the meaning of words and phrases as they are used in a text, including figurative, connotative, and technical meanings.	10–47
Range of Reading and Level of Text Complexity	**Pages**
CCSS.ELA.RI.8.10. By the end of the year, read and comprehend literary nonfiction in the grades 6–8 text complexity band independently and proficiently.	10–47
Language Standards	
Conventions of Standard English	**Pages**
CCSS.ELA.L.8.1. Demonstrate command of the conventions of standard English grammar and usage when writing or speaking.	11–47
CCSS.ELA.L.8.2. Demonstrate command of the conventions of standard English capitalization, punctuation, and spelling when writing.	11–47
Knowledge of Language	**Pages**
CCSS.ELA.L.8.3. Use knowledge of language and its conventions when writing, speaking, reading, or listening.	10–47
Vocabulary Acquisition and Use	**Pages**
CCSS.ELA.L.8.4. Determine or clarify the meaning of unknown and multiple-meaning words and phrases based on *grade 8 reading and content*, choosing flexibly from a range of strategies.	10–47
CCSS.ELA.L.8.5. Demonstrate understanding of figurative language, word relationships, and nuances in word meanings.	10–47
CCSS.ELA.L.8.6. Acquire and use accurately grade-appropriate general academic and domain-specific words and phrases; gather vocabulary knowledge when considering a word or phrase important to comprehension or expression.	10–47
Writing Standards	
Production and Distribution of Writing	**Pages**
CCSS.ELA.W.8.4. Produce clear and coherent writing in which the development, organization, and style are appropriate to task, purpose, and audience.	10–47
Research to Build and Present Knowledge	**Pages**
CCSS.ELA.W.8.9. Draw evidence from literary or informational texts to support analysis, reflection, and research.	10–47

Multiple-Choice Test-Taking Tips

Some multiple-choice questions are straightforward and easy. "I know the answer!" your brain yells right away. Some questions, however, stump even the most prepared student. In cases like that, you have to make an educated guess. An educated guess is a guess that uses what you know to help guide your attempt. You don't put your hand over your eyes and pick a random letter! You select it because you've thought about the format of the question, the word choice, the other possible answers, and the language of what's being asked. By making an educated guess, you're increasing your chances of guessing correctly. Whenever you are taking a multiple-choice assessment, you should remember to follow the rules below:

1. Read the directions. It's crucial. You may assume you know what is being asked, but sometimes directions can be tricky when you least expect them to be.

2. Read the questions before you read the passage. Doing this allows you to read the text through a more educated and focused lens. For example, if you know that you will be asked to identify the main idea, you can be on the lookout for that ahead of time.

3. Don't skip a question. Instead, try to make an educated guess. That starts with crossing off the ones you definitely know are not the correct answer. For instance, if you have four possible answers (A, B, C, D) and you can cross off two of them immediately, you've doubled your chances of guessing correctly. If you don't cross off any obvious ones, you would only have a 25% chance of guessing right. However, if you cross off two, you now have a 50% chance!

4. Read carefully for words like *always*, *never*, *not*, *except*, and *every*. Words like these are there to make you stumble. They make the question very specific. Sometimes an answer can be right some of the time, but if a word like *always* or *every* is in the question, the answer must be right *all of the time.*

5. After reading a question, try to come up with the answer first in your head before looking at the possible answers. That way, you will be less likely to bubble or click something you aren't sure about.

6. In questions with an "All of the Above" answer, think of it this way: if you can identify at least two that are correct, then "All of the Above" is probably the correct answer.

7. In questions with a "None of the Above" answer, think of it this way: if you can identify at least two that are *not* correct, then "None of the Above" is probably the correct answer.

8. Don't keep changing your answer. Unless you are sure you made a mistake, usually the first answer you chose is the right one.

Racing Into History

Danica Patrick is one of the most successful racecar drivers in the world. However, what makes her really special is that she is one of only a few women who race cars professionally. Danica was born on March 25, 1982, in Wisconsin. She first began racing go-carts with her sister at the age of 10. When she grew up, she began to pursue more serious car races.

The Indianapolis 500 is one of racing's most prestigious events. This means that it is a well-respected event. In 2005, Danica took part in this prestigious race. She was only the fourth woman to ever do that. She came in fourth place. No woman had ever done so well in this race.

In 2013, she won the time trials at the Daytona 500. A time trial is when a racer speeds his or her car around the track and tries to beat the best time. The winner could then receive the pole position for the main race. The pole position is really important because it allows your car to start a race in the best spot on the track. Danica became the first woman to ever win the pole position for the Daytona 500. She later raced across the finish line to win eighth place in the highly competitive race.

Danica's ability has earned her many awards. It has also provided her with other opportunities. She has appeared in many commercials, music videos, and television shows. She's even published a book about her life.

Despite her success in the racecar industry, Danica won't be satisfied until she wins. "I was brought up to be the fastest driver, not the fastest girl," she said.

Answer the following questions about the story "Racing Into History." The weights show you how hard you will need to work to find each answer.

1. In what year did Danica Patrick first race the Indianapolis 500?

   Ⓐ 1982   Ⓒ 2005

   Ⓑ 1905   Ⓓ 2013

2. What does it mean that it was a "highly competitive race"?

   Ⓐ It was raised off the ground.

   Ⓑ Everyone was trying hard to win.

   Ⓒ It was really expensive to race.

   Ⓓ It was a complicated event.

3. What does the word *prestigious* mean?

   Ⓐ well-respected   Ⓒ impressive

   Ⓑ frowned upon   Ⓓ famous

4. How do you infer Danica felt after winning the pole position for the Daytona 500?

   Ⓐ frightened

   Ⓑ unhappy

   Ⓒ brave

   Ⓓ proud

On the lines below, write your own question based on "Racing Into History." Circle the correct picture on the left to show the level of the question you wrote.

_____

_____

_____

_____

═══════════════════════════════════════

On a separate piece of paper . . .

- Write a sentence that includes the word *pursue*.

- If you were a famous athlete, what other opportunities would you pursue? Would you be in commercials or television shows? Name some things you think you might do.

═══════════════════════════════════════

An Oddly Delicious Fruit

A cherimoya (chair-uh-MOY-yuh) fruit might look prehistoric, but it is considered by many people today to be delicious. Scientists think these fruits originated in Ecuador and other nearby lands. Ecuador is a South American country whose name is Spanish for "equator." Over time, people brought cherimoyas to Asia and Spain.

Cherimoyas grow on shrubby, low-branched trees. The heart-shaped fruit is about 4–8 inches long and 4 inches wide, and it can weigh about a pound. However, some may weigh as much as five or six pounds. These exotic fruits are cultivated in California for specialty grocery markets. They are in season from January to April, depending on temperatures. Cherimoyas do best in regions with climates similar to those found in temperate coastal areas.

Scientists have studied how cherimoya trees pollinate and produce fruit. It's a tricky process, as flowers first bloom as female and then become male within several hours. In native environments, beetles help carry pollen. Growers pollinate by hand in commercial groves, harvesting pollen from open male flowers in the evening and applying it to female blossoms in the morning.

The flesh of a cherimoya is ivory-colored, with a custard-like consistency. Cherimoyas have green skin with a golden tint. If there is some brown, that's okay. Generally, cherimoya is ripe and ready to eat about seven days after it is picked. Avoid fruit that is black or shriveled, and do not eat the skin or the seeds. These parts are inedible and can cause severe health problems if ingested.

People think a cherimoya tastes like a blend of tropical fruits such as banana, coconut, and mango. The fruit is a good source of potassium and vitamin C. It also has fiber and other vitamins and minerals. The easiest way to taste this fruit is to cut it in half and spoon out the flesh. Remember, don't eat the large black seeds! Cherimoya fruit may also be added to smoothies or used to make fruit salad.

Answer the following questions about the story "An Oddly Delicious Fruit." The weights show you how hard you will need to work to find each answer.

1. Which statement best describes the native environment of cherimoyas?

    Ⓐ They originated in Asia and Spain.
    Ⓑ They thrive in the far north.
    Ⓒ They are native to the United States.
    Ⓓ They originated in South America near the equator.

2. A cherimoya is sometimes described as the "ice cream fruit." What can you infer from the passage that would support this opinion?

    Ⓐ It is processed and frozen like ice cream.
    Ⓑ It is a sweet-tasting food.
    Ⓒ Scooping out the custard-like flesh with a spoon is like eating ice cream.
    Ⓓ People eat cherimoyas only as a dessert.

3. Which of these is not given as being found in a cherimoya?

    Ⓐ vitamin C   Ⓑ fiber   Ⓒ potassium   Ⓓ protein

4. Which of these statements can you infer from the information given in the passage?

    Ⓐ Cherimoyas shouldn't be picked until they are fully ripe.
    Ⓑ The cherimoya's flesh is often brown.
    Ⓒ The cherimoya's seeds could be dangerous to eat.
    Ⓓ The cherimoya's skin has a custard-like consistency.

On the lines below, write your own question based on "An Oddly Delicious Fruit." Circle the correct picture on the left to show the level of the question you wrote.

_____

_____

_____

_____

On a separate piece of paper . . .

- Write a sentence that uses the word *cultivated*.
- Describe what you would need to know if you wanted to grow cherimoyas to sell commercially.

A Thrilling Ride

Many people have a fascination with roller coasters. What attracts us to this particular amusement-park ride? Designers incorporate factors such as gravity, acceleration, and an awareness of what people fear to create a ride that thrills.

The scientific principle that drives a coaster is the transfer of potential energy to kinetic energy. The potential energy is based on the height of the first hill. The higher the object ascends, the more potential energy is built up. When the coaster starts to go down the hill, potential energy becomes kinetic energy. This type of energy propels the coaster through the track. It builds and carries the cars up subsequent hills, thus creating additional potential energy. The ascents and descents, along with the shifts between potential energy and kinetic energy, result in changes in speed. This adds to the excitement of the ride.

Individual components of a roller coaster contribute to the overall ride. Running wheels keep the coaster on track while friction wheels control the lateral motion. An additional set of wheels keep the coaster on track even if inverted. Compressed-air brakes halt the machine at the end of the ride. Roller coasters generally are constructed out of one of two types of material: wood or steel. Coasters made of steel can travel higher, faster, and incorporate loops. Wood coasters usually aren't inverted, don't have loops, and don't travel with as great a speed. So what makes wooden coasters especially thrilling? They sway more. The rickety feel of the track increases the thrill of the ride.

Why do we feel a roller coaster is thrilling? As gravity pulls us down, we feel the upward pressure of the ground, or the weight beneath us (in this case, the roller coaster car). Another force that affects us is the acceleration. As the coaster speeds up and slows down, we feel pressure from different directions. The movement of our bodies is separate from that of the roller-coaster car. As the machine changes speed or direction, it acts as a force to change our motion. We don't fully understand these forces, which only adds to the excitement as our bodies experience the unknown for each twist and turn of the ride.

Answer the following questions about the story "A Thrilling Ride." The weights show you how hard you will need to work to find each answer.

1. Which of these is *not* true about steel roller coasters in relation to wooden coasters?

Ⓐ They are faster.

Ⓑ They can incorporate loops.

Ⓒ They are more rickety.

Ⓓ They can go higher.

2. In this passage, what does the word *lateral* mean?

Ⓐ forward

Ⓑ side to side

Ⓒ reverse

Ⓓ parallel

3. How does the last paragraph contribute to the main idea?

Ⓐ It explains the history of roller coasters.

Ⓑ It explains how to design and build a roller coaster.

Ⓒ It explains how roller coasters work.

Ⓓ It explains how the physics of roller coasters affects people.

4. From the information given in the passage, what is true about potential energy?

Ⓐ A low hill gives a roller coaster more potential energy than a high one.

Ⓑ A roller coaster has its most potential energy when it is stopped.

Ⓒ Since a steel roller coaster can have higher hills, it can build more potential energy.

Ⓓ Compressed-air brakes increase the potential energy at the end of the ride.

On the lines below, write your own question based on "A Thrilling Ride." Circle the correct picture on the left to show the level of the question you wrote.

_____

_____

_____

_____

___

On a separate piece of paper . . .

- Write a sentence that uses the word *kinetic*.

- How could the principle of transferring potential energy to kinetic energy be applied to something you experience in every day life?

___

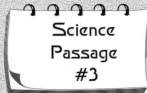
The Sleep Hormone

Have you ever tried going to bed when you felt tired and then tried waking up without an alarm clock? Melatonin is a natural hormone. Our bodies produce this chemical in glands. It helps our bodies know when it's nighttime and when it's time to get up. The brain controls levels of the hormone, which rise in the evening and decrease in the early morning. In this way, the brain signals the body to sleep and wake up. Light affects how much melatonin our bodies produce. Some people experience different levels of melatonin in the winter months, when the days are shorter. Their hormone levels may change at different times of the day. This causes changes in their sleeping and waking habits, which in turn affects how alert they feel.

Our natural sleeping and waking rhythms can be thrown off by artificial light from indoor lighting and electronic devices, such as TVs and computers. The additional light stops levels of melatonin from rising as early as they should. In the morning, we prepare for the day indoors and often go directly to school or work, not giving our bodies enough natural light to fully wake up. Melatonin levels don't drop as quickly, leaving us feeling groggy.

Researchers have studied what happens when people spend more time outdoors, for example, camping. Over a period of time, their body clocks reset so that they wake over an hour earlier than normal. They also go to bed earlier than they had previously. There are other ways to help reset your body clock, making it easier to wake up and feel alert in the mornings. Go for a morning walk or open the window shades or curtains to let in as much natural light as possible. Spend some time outdoors by walking to the bus stop or asking to be dropped off a few blocks from school and walking the rest of the way.

The role melatonin plays is just one factor in our quality of sleep, an activity required by our brains and our bodies for overall well-being. Balancing the amount of natural light we get with the artificial light in our environment is one way we can feel alert and do our best each day.

Answer the following questions about the story "The Sleep Hormone." The weights show you how hard you will need to work to find each answer.

1. Based on what you read in the passage, what might you infer about people's melatonin levels in the summer, when the days are longer and people spend more time outside?

   Ⓐ Melatonin levels would decrease, changing their waking and sleeping patterns.

   Ⓑ People would feel groggy because their bodies would produce more melatonin.

   Ⓒ Their bodies would produce more melatonin, which would give them more energy.

   Ⓓ People would wake up earlier and go to bed later.

2. Which is an example of something that gives off artificial light?

   Ⓐ TV   Ⓑ sun   Ⓒ computer   Ⓓ both A and C

3. Which best describes the relationship between melatonin levels and natural light?

   Ⓐ People who are not exposed to natural light do not sleep.

   Ⓑ If we get enough natural light, our bodies do not need to produce melatonin.

   Ⓒ Melatonin levels are not affected by natural light.

   Ⓓ Natural light keeps melatonin levels normal.

4. What did researchers discover about people who spent more time outdoors?

   Ⓐ They got tired more easily.   Ⓒ They produced less melatonin.

   Ⓑ They woke up earlier.   Ⓓ They needed less artificial light.

On the lines below, write your own question based on "The Sleep Hormone." Circle the correct picture on the left to show the level of the question you wrote.

_____

_____

_____

_____

On a separate piece of paper . . .

• Write a sentence that uses the word *natural*.

• How would it affect people's melatonin levels if they lived in a place where the sun does not shine very often but they went outside every day anyway?

The World's Wildest Weather

Many people have an interest in the weather forecast. It helps us decide whether or not we'll need an umbrella or snow boots. More than the daily forecast, reports of extreme weather often catch our attention. If our local forecast includes an extreme-weather warning, we plan what to do to prepare in case of emergency. Sometimes it's fascinating to learn about extreme weather in other places, where it might not affect us quite as much.

The National Weather Service keeps records of temperature, wind, precipitation, and other data from stations around the country. One place stands out as having extreme weather compared to other locations. Mount Washington, New Hampshire, holds several extreme-weather records. This area has the average coldest temperature in the contiguous United States. It receives the most rain and the most snow. Imagine, over 100 inches of rain and over 200 inches of snow a year! It comes as no surprise that the mountain also has the greatest number of cloudy days per year. The total number of days with precipitation is almost equal to the total number of cloudy days. In other words, most of the time when it's cloudy, it rains or snows. It also ranks second in levels of humidity. Until recently, the summit held the record for the highest wind gust recorded on Earth's surface at 231 mph!

Most of Mount Washington itself is part of White Mountain National Forest, with the summit located in Mount Washington State Park. A private, nonprofit observatory records weather conditions and conducts scientific research. State park crew and observatory staff live on the summit year round.

Three major storm tracks come together at the summit. This geographic location plays a role in the mountain's extreme weather. The steep slopes cause winds to pick up speed as they rise up from the valleys. As the highest point in the surrounding mountain range, it gets the worst of any storms that come through.

Weather observations from the summit are transmitted to the National Weather Service. Studying extreme weather helps us understand all types of weather better.

Name: _____   Science Passage #4

Answer the following questions about the story "The World's Wildest Weather." The weights show you how hard you will need to work to find each answer.

1. What causes Mount Washington's extreme weather?

Ⓐ the elevation of the mountain   Ⓒ geographic location

Ⓑ steep slopes   Ⓓ all of the above

2. In this passage, what does *precipitation* mean?

Ⓐ rain or snow that falls to the ground   Ⓒ the highest recorded gust of wind

Ⓑ the area near the summit of a mountain   Ⓓ the recording of weather conditions

3. Which of these facts is the least important to the main idea of the story?

Ⓐ Until recently, the summit held the record for the highest wind gust recorded on Earth's surface at 231 mph.

Ⓑ Three major storm tracks come together at the summit.

Ⓒ State park crew and observatory staff live on the summit year round.

Ⓓ Mount Washington, New Hampshire, holds several weather records.

4. In which of these places did a 231 mph gust of wind *not* occur?

Ⓐ New Hampshire   Ⓒ White Mountain National Forest

Ⓑ the summit of Mount Washington   Ⓓ Mount Washington State Park

On the lines below, write your own question based on "The World's Wildest Weather." Circle the correct picture on the left to show the level of the question you wrote.

_____

_____

_____

_____

On a separate piece of paper . . .

• Write a sentence that includes the word *transmitted*.

• How do you think your community's weather compares to Mount Washington? Think about temperature, precipitation, cloud cover, and wind as you explain your answer.

©*Teacher Created Resources*   19   *#3833 Nonfiction Reading Comprehension*

A Code for Health

What is DNA? Our cells contain two types of acids. DNA is the acid that controls the function of each cell. It's like a computer code that programs a computer. DNA has four chemical bases, which are referred to by their first letter. The chemical bases adenine (A) and thymine (T) pair up together. The other two chemical bases, guanine (G) and cytosine (C), also form pairs. These combinations are called base pairs. Each pair attaches to a sugar molecule and a phosphate molecule. Together, they form a nucleotide. Nucleotides form two long strands together in a double helix, or spiral. You may have seen a drawing of a DNA double helix. It looks like a ladder, with the base pairs forming the rungs and the sugar and phosphate molecules forming the vertical spines.

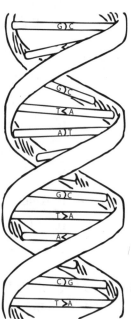

The sequence of base pairs makes up a gene. A gene is a combination of pieces of DNA code, or combinations of base pairs. Base pairs cluster together in groups of three. These groups of three combine to form a genetic sequence. Genes instruct cells to make specific protein molecules. Proteins carry out a variety of functions in the body.

The genes we inherit from our parents determine our physical traits and characteristics. Genes interact with the environment, which also affects the ways in which physical traits are expressed. Two organisms may have the same DNA, as in identical twins (animal or human). However, environmental differences such as diet can cause chemical clusters near genes to switch on and off. This results in observable differences in size, coloring, or other characteristics.

Scientists study DNA to learn how species survive and adapt to changes in the environment. As they continue to learn more about DNA and genetic inheritance, their research provides important information about inherited conditions and treatment.

Answer the following questions about the story "A Code for Health." The weights show you how hard you will need to work to find each answer.

1. What do some people compare the structure of DNA to?

Ⓐ beads and string   Ⓒ a ladder

Ⓑ a chain link fence   Ⓓ a jungle gym

2. How many chemical bases combine to form a DNA?

Ⓐ two   Ⓒ four

Ⓑ three   Ⓓ seven

3. According to the passage, what is one cause of differences between organisms with identical DNA?

Ⓐ genetic mutations   Ⓒ scientific research about DNA

Ⓑ having different parents   Ⓓ what the organisms eat

4. How does DNA help organisms adapt to changes in their environment?

Ⓐ The chemicals in genes are no longer active.

Ⓑ Factors in the environment can cause changes in genes.

Ⓒ Physical traits are always expressed the same, so organisms always have the same ability to survive.

Ⓓ The changes do not affect the physical characteristics of an organism.

On the lines below, write your own question based on "A Code for Health." Circle the correct picture on the left to show the level of the question you wrote.

_____

_____

_____

_____

On a separate piece of paper . . .

- Write a sentence that uses the word *inherited*.

- What do you think would happen if identical twins lived their lives in exactly the same ways— ate the same food, slept the same amount of time, played the same sports, etc.? Give evidence for your conclusion(s).

Folly or Investment?

When we think of states joining the Union, pioneers and frontier territories may come to mind. We also may remember reading about the Louisiana Purchase and how it added land to the Union. In these ways and more, the first 48 states became part of the United States and formed one cohesive country. But there are two states that do not share boundaries with any of the other states. Alaska and Hawaii, the last two states to join the Union, are not part of the contiguous United States. The United States purchased Alaska as a parcel of land.

Originally, Alaska was part of Russia. During the nineteenth century, Russia had war debts and was unable to adequately defend the area. This led Russia to seek a buyer for the land. During secret negotiations, the Russian minister to the United States agreed to sell the parcel to the United States for over seven million dollars. That might not seem like much money for a large amount of land today, but at the time, many people thought it a foolish decision. Secretary of State William H. Seward agreed to the purchase. People called it "Seward's Folly." The land was mostly unexplored, but people knew it was cold. They referred to it as "Seward's icebox" or President Johnson's "polar bear garden." Prevailing opinion was that nothing worthwhile grew or lived there. Seward thought the purchase of Alaska would be a good investment. It was a huge amount of land and would increase the size of the United States by almost 20 percent. Russia had offered to sell earlier, but issues within our government delayed final approvals.

Although Alaska didn't become a state for almost 100 years after the purchase, Seward was correct in his thinking. Within 20 years, gold was discovered in Alaska. Later, people found oil, an important natural resource. A variety of wildlife makes its home there, and vast forest lands provide additional natural resources. Alaska has proven to be far from a "folly."

Answer the following questions about the story "Folly or Investment?" The weights show you how hard you will need to work to find each answer.

1. Which evidence is irrelevant to the main idea?

Ⓐ The parcel of land increased the size of the United States by almost 20 percent.

Ⓑ Gold was discovered in Alaska shortly after the purchase.

Ⓒ Alaska didn't become a state for almost 100 years after the purchase.

Ⓓ The state continues to contribute to our country's economy.

2. Judging by how it is used in the passage, what is a synonym for the word *folly*?

Ⓐ mistake   Ⓒ purchase

Ⓑ resource   Ⓓ boundary

3. The passage implies that the main reason Alaska has been a good investment is

Ⓐ the state pays the United States money.

Ⓑ the state is rich in natural resources.

Ⓒ the purchase was a peaceful agreement between the United States and Russia.

Ⓓ Seward helped pay for the land.

4. What about Alaska made people think is was not worth buying?

Ⓐ harsh climate   Ⓒ abundance of plant and animal life

Ⓑ inadequate roads   Ⓓ discovery of gold

On the lines below, write your own question based on "Folly or Investment?" Circle the correct picture on the left to show the level of the question you wrote.

_____

_____

_____

_____

On a separate piece of paper . . .

• Write a sentence that uses the word *cohesive*.

• If you were debating for or against the purchase of Alaska, which position would you take? Why?

War on the Home Front

"Japanese Make Direct Hit on Oil Field Near Santa Barbara." Does this headline surprise you? It illustrates the fact that often during wartime, news is repressed. Some other events may not be widely reported for political reasons or because they are not deemed newsworthy.

On February 23, 1942, a Japanese submarine surfaced and shelled an oil field north of Santa Barbara, California. The attack caused only minor damage to property and no injuries. However, the event created a fear of invasion among those living along the California coast.

The attack began at 7:16 pm, during a presidential fireside chat. These talks by U.S. President Franklin D. Roosevelt were broadcast nationally over the radio. The sub fired a total of 16 shells. Three shells struck near an oil refinery, the apparent target of the attack. A shell destroyed rigging and pumping equipment. Two other shells landed on ranches but didn't cause damage. One person was wounded trying to defuse an unexploded shell. The remaining shells fell short and landed in the ocean.

What prompted the attack? Some accounts claim the submarine captain sought revenge for an incident a few years earlier. Following the attack, the United States increased defenses along the Pacific coastline.

A few months later, the United States attacked Japanese home islands. Japan responded by sending long-range submarines across the Pacific. The original goal was to raid shipping along the coast. A submarine shelled a lighthouse on Vancouver Island and another attacked a Canadian freighter. The second sub moved closer to shore to avoid minefields around the Columbia River. On June 21, 1942, the Japanese submarine fired a deck gun at the shore at Fort Stevens in Oregon. Permission was never granted to return fire, as the vessel was inaccurately determined to be out of range. The commander also claimed he did not want to give away the fort's defensive position. The shells left craters on the beach and damaged a power line.

There is inconclusive evidence for the cause of the first attack in Santa Barbara. However, the attack at Fort Stevens is recorded as the only hostile shelling of a military base on the U.S. mainland during World War II.

Name: _____

Answer the following questions about the story "War on the Home Front." The weights show you how hard you will need to work to find each answer.

1. What does the story say happened during the attack at Fort Stevens?

    Ⓐ A Japanese submarine attacked Vancouver Island.

    Ⓑ An attack occurred during a presidential fireside chat.

    Ⓒ The commander did not give permission to return fire.

    Ⓓ The Japanese attacked Santa Barbara.

2. What do the two attacks have in common?

    Ⓐ Each attack was a hostile attack by the enemy.

    Ⓑ Return fire was ordered by a commander.

    Ⓒ A Japanese submarine fired shells at an oil field.

    Ⓓ Both attacks made major news headlines.

3. A repressed news story is one that is

    Ⓐ withheld.   Ⓑ pressed again.   Ⓒ featured.   Ⓓ reported.

4. What was one important result of the attack on Santa Barbara?

    Ⓐ The submarine captain wanted revenge.

    Ⓑ The United States increased defenses along the Pacific coastline.

    Ⓒ Several shells landed in the ocean.

    Ⓓ The target of the attack was a ranch.

On the lines below, write your own question based on "War on the Home Front." Circle the correct picture on the left to show the level of the question you wrote.

_____

_____

_____

_____

On a separate piece of paper . . .

- Write a sentence that uses the word *deemed*.

- What is your evaluation of the commander's decision to not allow return fire? Explain.

Our Valuable Money

People have used money, or currency, for trading for thousands of years. By the time the United States declared independence from Britain, coins were in widespread use. The new country needed its own monetary system separate from Britain. The Coinage Act of 1792 established the first U.S. Mint. Before that time, people used foreign and colonial currency, livestock, produce, and wampum (beads made from shells) for commerce. In those early days, most coins were made from precious metals such as gold or silver. The Act of 1792 established certain denominations of coins to be made of gold. At that time, America had $10, $5, and $2.50 gold coins. Coins of lesser values were to be made of silver. Silver coins included dollar, half-dollar, and half-dime coins, as well as quarters and dimes. Minor coins, such as the penny and half penny, were made of copper.

It didn't take long for criminals to begin shaving small bits from the gold and silver coins. They sold the precious metals for profit. Within a few short years, the process of making coins changed to prevent criminal activity, including counterfeiting. The new process, called *reeding*, put grooves on the edges of coins. Different denominations of coin have different numbers of grooves, or reeds. The coin with the highest number of reeds is the silver American Eagle one-ounce dollar. Other coins that have reeding include the dime, quarter, and half dollar. Most coins have between 100–200 individual reeds. Criminals could no longer shave the edges without the result being obvious.

Today, none of our coins contain precious metals. President Roosevelt ordered the cessation of production of gold coins during the Great Depression. Since the silver crisis in the 1960s, coins are no longer made of silver either. However, our coins still have ridges. Why? The ridges on some coins make it easier for sight-impaired people to tell the difference between similar-sized coins. Reeds on coins also make them more intricate and difficult to counterfeit.

Answer the following questions about the story "Our Valuable Money." The weights show you how hard you will need to work to find each answer.

1. What is the process called that puts grooves on the edges of coins?

Ⓐ shaving   Ⓑ reeding   Ⓒ coinage   Ⓓ counterfeiting

2. Which statement does not describe a purpose of reeding?

Ⓐ It makes it easier to create unique coin designs.

Ⓑ It stops criminals from shaving small bits of precious metal to sell.

Ⓒ It makes counterfeiting more difficult.

Ⓓ It helps visually-impaired people tell coins apart.

3. What does the word *counterfeit* mean as used in this passage?

Ⓐ to create a duplicate image

Ⓑ to make an imitation of something genuine in order to defraud

Ⓒ to pretend

Ⓓ to resemble something closely

4. How does the second paragraph contribute to the main idea?

Ⓐ It describes criminal activity.

Ⓑ It describes the history of money.

Ⓒ It describes a process that makes it more difficult to devalue our money.

Ⓓ It describes how to make counterfeit money.

On the lines below, write your own question based on "Our Valuable Money." Circle the correct picture on the left to show the level of the question you wrote.

_____

_____

_____

_____

On a separate piece of paper . . .

• Write a sentence that includes the word *currency*.

• Look closely at a coin. Write down everything you notice about it.

Vending Machines

A part of the American landscape, vending machines first came into widespread use in the late 1800s. A vending machine is a device that dispenses goods for currency. By this definition, amusement park games and music machines are not vending machines. Vending machines offer the consumer the convenience of time and place.

However, the first vending machine was invented earlier than we might think. In the first century A.D., Hero of Alexandria devised a machine to dispense Holy Water. The machine operated on simple physics principles. A consumer dropped a coin into a slot on top of a box. The coin struck a lever with a string attached to the other end of the lever. The string is tied to a stopper that plugs a container of liquid. When the lever is struck by the coin, it lifts the other end with the string and removes the plug. The liquid pours out until the coin drops off the end of the lever. Early vending machines used similar technology before widespread use of electrical machines.

One of the first uses of vending machines was to sell stamps. Another early purpose was for retailers to get their products, such as chewing gum, into places they could not otherwise sell. Early vending machines appeared on railway platforms. For several years, industry expansion was limited mostly to penny candy sales. In the 1930s, soft drink machines appeared. The industry expanded to include other types of food as the country geared up for wartime production. Managers in factories figured people could not work the required long shifts without a refreshment break. Vending machines offered a practical way to meet the need. For the next two decades, vending machines continued to be used mainly in factories. When refrigeration was added to machines, it became possible to sell fresh foods and cold beverages.

Owners of vending machines, called operators, place their machines on property owned by others, such as on a college campus or in a healthcare facility. These operators provide all maintenance and products needed for the machines. Sometimes there may be a service charge to the property owner, but often there is no cost.

Today we see vending machines in a wide variety of locations. This invention makes it possible for people to purchase items at competitive prices any time of day, any day of the year.

Answer the following questions about the story "Vending Machines." The weights show you how hard you will need to work to find each answer.

1. In the first vending machine, which of these happened first?

   Ⓐ The machine dispensed liquid.   Ⓒ The lever lifted the string.

   Ⓑ The coin struck a lever.   Ⓓ The string removed the plug.

2. Which statement does not describe a benefit of vending machines?

   Ⓐ Vending machines offer consumers convenience.

   Ⓑ Vending machines offer competitive prices.

   Ⓒ It is easy for operators to maintain the machines.

   Ⓓ Vending machines make it easy for people to have a refreshment break.

3. Which is *not* mentioned as something an operator needs to provide?

   Ⓐ the machine   Ⓒ products

   Ⓑ maintenance   Ⓓ service charge

4. Which of these statements is the least relevant to the main idea?

   Ⓐ Amusement park games and music machines are not vending machines.

   Ⓑ One of the first uses of vending machines was to sell stamps.

   Ⓒ Today we see vending machines in a wide variety of places.

   Ⓓ Vending machines offer the consumer the convenience of time and place.

On the lines below, write your own question based on "Vending Machines." Circle the correct picture on the left to show the level of the question you wrote.

_____

_____

_____

_____

On a separate piece of paper . . .

- Write a sentence that uses the word *retailers*.

- Design a vending machine. Describe what it would offer and list the intended consumer market.

The History of Fashion

What is fashion? One international fashion writer claims it is a state of mind. People create their own sense of style based on their self-perception. Every day we make choices about what to wear. Our choices reflect our planned activities for the day, as well as our emotions. The clothes we wear tell others a little bit about us.

We make our clothing choices based on several factors. Weather impacts what we wear, as do the activities we have planned for the day. Through our clothing, we might wish to convey a message, or we might dress to appear attractive to others. We make choices based on our moods; for example, you might have a favorite top or pair of jeans you wear when you're having a great day. The concept of "what's in style" changes constantly. We receive new ideas from television, movies, and advertisements.

Many prominent people influence our sense of fashion. People in the entertainment industry, such as musicians and actors, often set trends. Political figures and royalty also play a role. Throughout history, people have looked to popular and political figures for fashion. Hundreds of years ago, people outside large cities relied on sketches to learn about what famous people wore. Throughout history, people in different groups have dressed differently. You could tell if someone was a peasant or royalty by the clothes they wore. Often clothing may be the first distinguishing feature.

Today, some people choose their clothing to identify with a particular group, such as "goth" or "prep." Even though clothing can aid in including someone in a group, it can also create distance between groups. For instance, a business executive might not listen as carefully to someone perceived by their clothing to be in a completely different social group. Some religious groups dictate certain aspects of members' clothing to identify with that group and its beliefs. People in certain occupations may have clothing that is part of the job, for example, the robes a judge wears or the uniform a police officer wears.

A famous person may make a fashion statement, but it takes individuals to react to events to move a style into popular culture. The concept of style has been part of our world for hundreds of years, and although it will change, fashion won't disappear.

Answer the following questions about the story "The History of Fashion." The weights show you how hard you will need to work to find each answer.

1. To which groups of people would you compare peasants and royalty today?

    Ⓐ servants and masters   Ⓒ students and teachers

    Ⓑ laborers and executives   Ⓓ presidents and kings

2. Finish this analogy: **perceive : perception** as _____.

    Ⓐ **president : politician**   Ⓒ **execute : executive**

    Ⓑ **royalty : revolution**   Ⓓ **popular : fashion**

3. Which statement best summarizes the main idea?

    Ⓐ Fashion expresses a person's identity.

    Ⓑ Famous people dictate fashion and what we should wear.

    Ⓒ People have no choice over which group they identify with.

    Ⓓ History tells us what is in style.

4. Which of these is not mentioned as something you might be able to tell about a person by what he or she is wearing?

    Ⓐ what job he or she has

    Ⓑ what type of music he or she likes

    Ⓒ how much money he or she has

    Ⓓ if he or she is a nice person

On the lines below, write your own question based on "The History of Fashion." Circle the correct picture on the left to show the level of the question you wrote.

_____

_____

_____

_____

___

On a separate piece of paper . . .

- Write a sentence that uses the word *prominent*.

- In your opinion, how can learning about the history of fashion benefit us today?

René Descartes

If you've read a city or state map, you've used a simple version of the Cartesian coordinate system. René Descartes developed the concept of a coordinate plane. Born in the late 1500s in France, Descartes was raised by his grandmother and great uncle. He went to boarding school at age 8 and took the standard course of study, which included three years of mathematics. Some people speculate Descartes may have had poor health, as he didn't have to adhere to the school's rigorous schedule. His family wanted him to become a lawyer, following in the footsteps of his father and other relatives. Descartes did go to law school and obtained a degree, but he never practiced law. Instead, he joined the army. During that time, he met Dutch mathematician Isaac Beeckman, who became an influential teacher in Descartes' life. Descartes spent much of his later life in the Netherlands. The poor health of his youth persisted throughout his life, and he died of pneumonia at age 53 in Sweden.

Some people view Descartes as the father of modern philosophy. He took a different approach to philosophical questions, starting with a clean slate and the most basic statement of fact: I exist. This led him to the often-quoted statement "I think, therefore I am." He approached a study of the natural world through science and mathematics, seeking logic and order. His contributions to science and mathematics include the laws of refraction, which led to a greater understanding of rainbows. His development of the coordinate system forms the foundation of analytic algebra.

How does Descartes' coordinate system work? The x-axis crosses the y-axis at a 90-degree angle. Points are numbered along each axis, with values increasing as they move up and to the right. Values decrease as they move down and to the left. Legend has it that Descartes watched a fly on the ceiling one morning. He reasoned that the position of the fly could be determined by using a set of imagined points along each edge of the ceiling. At any specific location on the ceiling, the fly would be on or near the intersection of two points. He developed this theory into a system of coordinates we know as the Cartesian coordinate system.

Each era places René Descartes in a different category, but his work cannot be limited to one field or discovery. He's known as a mathematician, natural scientist, and philosopher. His developments and contributions continue to benefit us today.

Answer the following questions about the story "René Descartes." The weights show you how hard you will need to work to find each answer.

1. In what way is a map most like a coordinate plane?

Ⓐ Both have numbers and intersecting lines.

Ⓑ Both can be used to plot locations.

Ⓒ A fly might crawl across both surfaces.

Ⓓ Values decrease as one reads the map from left to right.

2. What does the word *refraction* mean as used in this passage?

Ⓐ the bending of a ray of light, which leads to the creation of rainbows

Ⓑ the bending of rays of light from a star

Ⓒ the ability of the eye to form an image on the retina

Ⓓ the degree to which light bends in a lens

3. Descartes is credited with saying, "I think, therefore I am." What might this mean?

Ⓐ All living creatures can think.

Ⓑ When we are asleep, we no longer exist.

Ⓒ One thing we know that is true is that Descartes could think.

Ⓓ You must exist in order to think about your existence.

4. Where did Descartes spend most of his later years?

Ⓐ the Netherlands   Ⓑ Sweden   Ⓒ the U.S.   Ⓓ France

On the lines below, write your own question based on "René Descartes." Circle the correct picture on the left to show the level of the question you wrote.

_____

_____

_____

_____

On a separate piece of paper . . .

• Write a sentence that uses the word *adhere*.

• The story says Descartes may have come up with an innovative idea while watching a fly. Is there a dull activity that helps you think creative thoughts? Explain.

César Chávez

Civil rights affect more than one group of people. César Chávez, a Mexican American, fought for labor rights for his people. Chávez was born in Arizona in 1927. His parents owned a ranch and a grocery store, but they lost everything in the Great Depression. Along with many other families, they moved to California, seeking work. César's family became migrant farm laborers, picking various crops in season. They moved from place to place, living in government camps at times. Farm workers earned low wages and experienced difficult living conditions. At times they didn't have access to clean water or bathrooms. Children often had to skip school to help work and earn wages for the family. César Chávez attended 30 schools and then was forced to quit in the eighth grade to care for his parents.

His past impacted how Chávez lived as an adult. With little education and training, he returned to farm work. But he felt the harsh conditions were wrong. He decided to organize migrant workers into a labor union. Chávez wanted to obtain higher wages and better working conditions for migrant workers. In 1962 he formed the National Farm Workers Association. Later, they joined with another union, the Agricultural Workers Organizing Committee. The merger became the United Farm Workers. A five-year labor strike in California led to support of the 1975 Agricultural Labor Relations Act. The act is a collective bargaining law for farm workers. Other nonviolent protest measures included marches and boycotts.

Chávez looked to other leaders for his ideas. He followed Martin Luther King Jr.'s example of nonviolent protest. Mahatma Gandhi of India inspired Chávez to fast to make his point. His peaceful tactics made it possible for farm workers to negotiate settlement contracts with growers. This resulted in better wages and treatment for migrant workers.

After his death in 1993, the president awarded César's widow the Medal of Freedom, the nation's highest civilian honor. Chávez's work didn't end with his death, however. As with other important historical figures, he had help along the way and the work he started continues. His legacy includes inspiring migrant workers to stand up for their rights and motivating Hispanic leaders to fight against discrimination.

Answer the following questions about the story "César Chávez." The weights show you how hard you will need to work to find each answer.

1. Which group formed from the merger of two labor unions?

    Ⓐ the Agricultural Farm Workers

    Ⓑ the National Farm Workers Association

    Ⓒ the United Farm Workers

    Ⓓ the Agricultural Workers Organizing Committee

2. What does the word *bargaining* mean as used in this passage?

    Ⓐ agreeing on what each side should do for or give to the other side

    Ⓑ agreeing to a fair price for a product

    Ⓒ trying to get something for nothing

    Ⓓ discussing wages and living conditions

3. Which Act provides for negotiations between growers and migrant farm workers?

    Ⓐ The Farm Workers Act   Ⓒ The Collective Bargaining Act

    Ⓑ The Medal of Freedom   Ⓓ The Agricultural Labor Relations Act

4. Which statement best summarizes the legacy of César Chávez?

    Ⓐ He led nonviolent protests against California growers.

    Ⓑ He inspired migrant farm workers to stand up for their rights.

    Ⓒ He has had streets and schools named after him.

    Ⓓ His widow received the Medal of Freedom.

On the lines below, write your own question based on "César Chávez." Circle the correct picture on the left to show the level of the question you wrote.

_____

_____

_____

_____

On a separate piece of paper . . .

• Write a sentence that uses the word *legacy*.

• How might nonviolent protest be more effective than using force? Explain your opinion.

J.R.R. Tolkien

Many people are familiar J.R.R. Tolkien's novels, most of which are set in a place called Middle-earth. Tolkien's fictional world is filled with unique inhabitants and made-up languages. But who was the man who created Middle-earth?

J.R.R. Tolkien was born to English parents in South Africa in 1892. He was named John Ronald Reuel, but his family just called him Ronald. After his father's death in 1896, Tolkien returned to England with his mother and younger brother. There, he split his growing-up years between a rural community south of Birmingham and the urban city itself. Ronald's mother died when he was 12. The family never had much money, and the parish priest took over the boys' upbringing. He boarded them at various places and made sure their needs were met.

Ronald did well in school, showing great aptitude in languages. He went on to college and pursued a degree in English literature. By this time he had begun to write stories, including those that would become part of a book called *Silmarillion*.

Following World War I, Tolkien secured a job at a university. He published academic works and was a co-founder of "The Inklings," a social group with an interest in writing. C.S. Lewis was also a member of the group and became one of Tolkien's closest friends. During this time, Ronald wrote stories for his children. One day, while marking exam papers, he scribbled something on the blank page at the end of an examination book. He wrote, "In a hole in the ground there lived a hobbit." This phrase caught his imagination and he began to develop the story, telling it to his children. As the story was passed around, a draft copy fell into the hands of an employee at a publishing company. She asked him to finish the tale. It met with the approval of the chairman of the firm, and it was published as *The Hobbit* in 1937. The success of the work led the publisher to ask for further stories. Tolkien submitted the tales he called *Silmarillion*, but they were not deemed publishable. Instead, Tolkien was asked to write a sequel to *The Hobbit*. Eventually *The Lord of the Rings* was published in three parts between 1954 and 1955. Although Tolkien wrote and published other works, he is best known for his fantastical tales of Middle-earth.

Answer the following questions about the story "J.R.R. Tolkien." The weights show you how hard you will need to work to find each answer.

1. How did Tolkien's aptitude for languages likely influence his writing?

   Ⓐ He understood language well enough to make up his own languages.

   Ⓑ He borrowed words from another language for his stories.

   Ⓒ It helped him learn English grammar.

   Ⓓ He set his stories in other countries.

2. How did *The Lord of the Rings* get published?

   Ⓐ Tolkien submitted it to several publishers.

   Ⓑ His family published it after his death.

   Ⓒ The publisher asked for a sequel to *The Hobbit.*

   Ⓓ His friends from "The Inklings" had it published.

3. Which other famous author belonged to the group "The Inklings?"

   Ⓐ George Bernard Shaw   Ⓒ G.K. Chesterton

   Ⓑ J.K. Rowling   Ⓓ C.S. Lewis

4. What is the most likely reason Tolkien's tales are described as "fantastical"?

   Ⓐ They are so distorted they do not make sense.

   Ⓑ They have highly imaginative characters and settings.

   Ⓒ They are extravagant and cost a lot of money.

   Ⓓ They are impossible and cannot exist.

On the lines below, write your own question based on "J.R.R. Tolkien." Circle the correct picture on the left to show the level of the question you wrote.

_____

_____

_____

_____

On a separate piece of paper . . .

- Write a sentence that uses the word *aptitude*.

- Think of a new world. Give your world a name and describe who lives there.

Admiral Hopper

When we think of people who have contributed to the computer industry, a major figure such as Bill Gates may come to mind. Admiral Grace Murray Hopper, a math professor should also be considered. After joining the U.S. Navy in 1943, she was stationed at Harvard. She worked on the Navy's Mark I, the first large-scale computer in the United States. She was one of the first to program the computer. Nearly 10 years later, she went on to invent a compiler. A computer compiler turns English commands into computer program code. This allows programmers to write code more easily and reduces the number of errors. Hopper later played a key role in developing COBOL. One of the first computer programming languages, COBOL stands for Common Business Oriented Language. Her work earned her the name "The Grand Lady of Software."

Admiral Hopper was born in New York in 1906. Grace's curiosity about gadgets began early in life. Imagine her delight, then, at being assigned to work on the Navy's Mark I. Her naval career spanned over 40 years, including assignments in research and computer programming. She earned a Ph.D. in mathematics from Yale University in 1934. In 1969 she received the Computer Sciences "Man of the Year" award. She was elected a member of the National Academy of Engineering in 1973. Later in life, she was awarded several honorary doctoral degrees for her work. These are just a few examples from an extensive list of awards and honors she received during her lifetime. Her career includes positions held as mathematics professor and senior mathematician. Hopper worked as a systems engineer and senior consultant, and she served many years of active duty in the Navy.

The story goes that Admiral Hopper was trying to track down an error on the Mark II. She traced the problem to a moth trapped in a relay. Once the moth was removed, it was taped into a daily log book. Now, whenever a computer has a problem, we refer to it as a "bug."

Quotes from Grace illustrate her philosophy in life. She said, "It's easier to ask forgiveness than to get permission." Hopper also believed that the most dangerous phrase in the language was "we've always done it this way." Her father encouraged her to go after what she wanted, and so she did.

Answer the following questions about the story "Admiral Hopper." The weights show you how hard you will need to work to find each answer.

1. Which accomplishment happened after Hopper received the "Man of the Year" award?

Ⓐ She joined the Navy.

Ⓑ She earned a Ph.D. in math.

Ⓒ She worked on the Mark I.

Ⓓ She was elected to the National Academy of Engineering.

2. Why do we call a computer problem a "bug?"

Ⓐ Bugs always get into computers.

Ⓑ It bugs us when computers break.

Ⓒ A moth got trapped in a computer.

Ⓓ Only small robots can fix it.

3. What can you infer about Grace Hopper's philosophy of life?

Ⓐ She was willing to try new things.

Ⓑ She didn't like to follow the rules.

Ⓒ She felt everyone had to do things the same way.

Ⓓ She believed only men could work on computers.

4. According to the passage, a computer compiler

Ⓐ puts the pages of code in the proper sequence.

Ⓑ turns English commands into computer code.

Ⓒ brings all the information the computer needs together in one place.

Ⓓ translates instructions from English to another language.

On the lines below, write your own question based on "Admiral Hopper." Circle the correct picture on the left to show the level of the question you wrote.

_____

_____

_____

_____

_____

_____

On a separate piece of paper . . .

• Write a sentence that uses the word *consultant*.

• What difference do Admiral Hopper's contributions make in our lives today?

Ultimate: The Game

There's Frisbee™… and then there's Ultimate. What makes this game so great? It's been around longer than you might think. Started in 1968 by a group of high school students, Ultimate uses athletic skills similar to other games. It incorporates the non-stop movement and endurance of soccer and the aerial passing skills of the football. Today, Ultimate is played in more than 80 countries around the world. There are national and international governing bodies. Since Ultimate doesn't require much in the way of equipment, it is easily accessible to many people.

The game is played with a flying disc, or Frisbee®. Two teams play on a field with end zones. Points are scored by catching a pass in the opponent's end zone. Players must stop running when holding the disc, but may pivot on one foot to pass. The game moves quickly, with the disc changing teams at several points. Possession of the disc changes teams when it is dropped or when one player holds the disc for longer than 10 seconds.

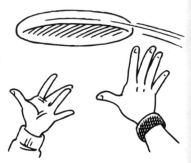

One aspect of the game that is very unique to Ultimate is that games are self-officiated, even at high levels. This is referred to in the sport as "Spirit of the Game." It places the responsibility for fair play back on the players, rather than referees. This develops sportsmanship, character, and conflict-resolution skills.

One of the primary goals of Ultimate is enjoyment of the game, including the challenge. Spirit of the Game contributes to this goal by encouraging players to settle disputes calmly, disrupting the game as little as possible. A list of 10 basic rules have been developed with the intent of keeping the game moving along when play is interrupted. Assuming no players would intentionally violate rules, guidelines establish how to resume play as if no infraction had occurred. Although players are encouraged to be competitive, Spirit of the Game relies on the concept that players will maintain respect for one another. Most Ultimate players take Spirit of the Game to heart, and that's what makes the system work. The core principle of Ultimate is the golden rule: treat others as you would like to be treated.

Answer the following questions about the story "Ultimate: The Game." The weights show you how hard you will need to work to find each answer.

1. In the game of Ultimate, what does "Spirit of the Game" mean?

   Ⓐ Treat the opposing players as they have treated you.

   Ⓑ Play competitively but with respect and enjoyment of the game.

   Ⓒ Make up your own rules as you go along.

   Ⓓ Encourage spectators to cheer for your team.

2. Which sport most closely compares to Ultimate?

   Ⓐ soccer   Ⓑ basketball   Ⓒ swimming   Ⓓ baseball

3. One goal of Ultimate is to

   Ⓐ make as many fouls as possible to hinder the opposing team.

   Ⓑ keep play moving as smoothly as possible.

   Ⓒ develop dribbling skills.

   Ⓓ get along with the referees.

4. What does it mean to say that the game of Ultimate is self-officiated?

   Ⓐ There is only one referee for the game.

   Ⓑ A player can make a call on someone else but not himself or herself.

   Ⓒ Everyone makes up his or her own rules for the game.

   Ⓓ Players enforce the rules of the game based on the honor system.

On the lines below, write your own question based on "Ultimate: The Game." Circle the correct picture on the left to show the level of the question you wrote.

_____

_____

_____

_____

_____

On a separate piece of paper . . .

 • Write a sentence that uses the word *infraction*.

 • How well do you think the honor system would work for self-officiating the game? Explain.

The Nobel Prizes

Alfred Nobel left a last will and testament. In it, he left most of his estate to be used as prizes in various academic areas. He said the prizes should be awarded to people who "during the preceding year, shall have conferred the greatest benefit to mankind." Alfred Nobel wanted to honor those who sought to bring good to our world. He established a way to acknowledge and reward such people for their efforts. What kind of person would do this?

Alfred Nobel was born in Sweden. His father was an engineer and inventor. Alfred's father moved to other countries as he tried to establish his business. Alfred and his brothers remained in Sweden with his mother. She used money from her side of the family to start a grocery store that supported them during this time. Later, the family moved to Russia to join Alfred's father. Alfred received private education and studied several languages, along with natural science and literature. His father discouraged his interest in literature, and Alfred went on to study chemical engineering. He later worked in Sweden developing nitroglycerine, an explosive. These experiments led to the invention of dynamite. He continued to develop inventions, and he acquired over 300 patents in his lifetime.

In his will, Nobel specified various categories for the prizes. He said prizes would be awarded in physics, chemistry, physiology or medicine, literature, and peace between nations. He sought discoveries, inventions, and work that benefited mankind as a whole. In keeping with that ideal, Alfred also said that candidates should be considered regardless of their nationality. Not everyone agreed with his plan for Nobel Prizes. It took four to five years after his death for the first prizes to be awarded.

Once a Nobel Prize has been awarded, it cannot be revoked. A committee carefully chooses each winner. That person may be chosen by majority vote, but the committee tries to reach complete consensus. The Nobel Prizes honor intellectual achievement. The winner receives over a million dollars. The amount of the award, as well as its history, contributes to its renown. Of the Prizes, many view the Nobel Prize as the "world's most prestigious prize."

Name: _____

Answer the following questions about the story "The Nobel Prizes." The weights show you how hard you will need to work to find each answer.

1. Which category was not mentioned in Alfred's will but added later as a Nobel Prize?

Ⓐ chemistry

Ⓑ literature

Ⓒ economics

Ⓓ physics

2. Which of the following is *not* a reason someone might be awarded a Nobel Prize?

Ⓐ graduating from college with honors

Ⓑ making an important discovery

Ⓒ inventing something that helps people

Ⓓ promoting peace between nations

3. Why are Nobel Prizes considered to be *prestigious* awards?

Ⓐ They motivate people to do better.

Ⓑ They have a reputation based on great achievement.

Ⓒ They are awarded to famous people.

Ⓓ The whole world knows about the prizes.

4. Which statement best summarizes Alfred Nobel's purpose in establishing Nobel Prizes?

Ⓐ He wanted to be famous.

Ⓑ He wanted the world to be a better place.

Ⓒ He wanted to leave his money to charity.

Ⓓ He wanted to create a committee that sought peace.

On the lines below, write your own question based on "The Nobel Prizes." Circle the correct picture on the left to show the level of the question you wrote.

_____

_____

_____

_____

====================================

On a separate piece of paper . . .

- Write a sentence that uses the word *consensus*.

- Who would you nominate for one of the Nobel Prizes? Specify which prize and give evidence and reasons for your decision.

Giving a Great Speech

It can be difficult to stand up and talk in front of people you don't know. Careful planning can make it easier and perhaps even enjoyable. There are two aspects to a great speech: content and delivery. Here are some pointers for preparing each:

Content

- If you have an assigned topic, find an aspect of that topic that interests you.
- Decide on a goal: What do you want your audience to take away or remember from your speech?
- Make an outline of major points you want to make.
- Include an attention-grabbing opening, solid information with sufficient evidence in the body, and a good conclusion that summarizes your main point(s).
- A fascinating anecdote, unusual fact, or interesting question can help get your audience's attention.
- Leave the audience with a thought or question to ponder.

Delivery

- Plan to put as much time into practicing your speech as you put into writing it.
- Memorize as much of your speech as possible.
- If needed, use note cards as reminders of your major points.
- Practice your speech at home in front of a mirror and time yourself.
- Consider using a visual aid if appropriate to the topic and assignment.
- Dress appropriately so your audience will take you seriously.
- Maintain eye contact with your audience. When you look at specific people in the audience, they will feel as if you are speaking directly to them.
- Be aware of your hands. Too many gestures will distract the audience.
- Speak more slowly and loudly than you would in a normal conversation.
- Stand up straight to show you are proud of what you have to say.

Answer the following questions about the story "Giving a Great Speech." The weights show you how hard you will need to work to find each answer.

1. What does the word *deliver* mean as it relates to a speech's delivery?

Ⓐ hand out   Ⓑ mail   Ⓒ throw   Ⓓ present

2. Which statement describes an appropriate thing to do when giving a speech?

Ⓐ Keep your hands in your pockets.

Ⓑ Speak quickly so your audience doesn't get bored.

Ⓒ Speak more slowly and loudly than you would in normal conversation.

Ⓓ Stare at your notes so you won't lose your place.

3. What is the author's opinion of giving a speech?

Ⓐ It is difficult to give a speech.

Ⓑ It can be enjoyable with proper planning.

Ⓒ Everyone has to give a speech during the school year.

Ⓓ The audience does not want to hear what the speaker has to say.

4. Why is it a good idea to choose an aspect of the topic that interests you?

Ⓐ It will be easier to research and focus your thoughts.

Ⓑ Your listeners will like your speech.

Ⓒ You won't have to practice your speech as much.

Ⓓ The audience will get to know your personality.

On the lines below, write your own question based on "Giving a Great Speech." Circle the correct picture on the left to show the level of the question you wrote.

_____

_____

_____

_____

On a separate piece of paper . . .

- Write a sentence that uses the word *gestures*.
- Why do you think it's important to develop good public speaking skills? How can such skills help you in other areas of life outside of school?

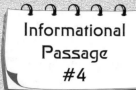

Designing a Skatepark

Have you ever wondered about the design process behind building an awesome skateboard park? Well, the first public skateparks used a variety of materials, such as concrete, wood, fiberglass, and steel. These materials formed the ramps and ledges for tricks. However, wood and steel deteriorate, requiring a lot of maintenance. This led cities to find another solution—concrete. Concrete lasts a long time with minimal wear and tear.

Designing a skatepark takes planning. In some communities, potential skatepark users are invited to participate in design meetings. Skateparks are described by size, as well as by the style of terrain. The smallest skateparks use an area of sidewalk or paved open space. They can support three to five skaters at a time. Large "regional" skateparks consist of 25,000 square feet or more. Most public skateparks parks fall in the mid-range of a "neighborhood" skatepark, between 6,000 and 10,000 square feet. These parks usually have clear boundaries indicating where the skating area begins and ends. They include a diverse array of features. Dozens of skaters can access the park, with up to six skating at one time.

Many different styles of skateparks exist. Features from one or more design styles may be found in a park. Skateable art refers to designs that are visually appealing to pedestrians. At the same time, they are "skate-friendly." For example, an arch might be incorporated into a sidewalk design. A street plaza park has features that might be found in an urban environment, such as ledges, stairs, or railing. Other features may include small green spaces, brick, or natural stone. Transition terrain has the halfpipes and bowls many people envision when they think of a skatepark. Today, more and more parks are featuring hybrid terrain. This is a combination of street plaza elements with transition terrain.

The hardest part of the process may be generating funding for a skatepark. Communities hold fundraisers and request donations. In some cases, skaters volunteer to help with the construction. Once built, skateparks must be maintained. For concrete parks, maintenance is minimal and consists mostly of concrete patching or repair. General facilities maintenance, including litter patrol, mirrors that of other public parks. It's safe to say that skateparks will be around for a while, providing interesting and safe places for skaters to practice their sport.

Answer the following questions about the story "Designing a Skatepark." The weights show you how hard you will need to work to find each answer.

1. Why might a skatepark include more than one type of terrain?

   Ⓐ It's easier to design and construct.

   Ⓑ It would appeal to a wider variety of skaters.

   Ⓒ It's more visually attractive.

   Ⓓ It's easier to maintain.

2. What is the first step in the process of designing a skateboard park?

   Ⓐ obtaining funding   Ⓒ constructing the park

   Ⓑ holding a design meeting   Ⓓ maintaining the park

3. According to the passage, which factor is not a consideration for skatepark designers?

   Ⓐ weather   Ⓒ type of terrain

   Ⓑ size   Ⓓ cost

4. What does the word *deteriorate* mean as used in this passage?

   Ⓐ lose value   Ⓒ become more expensive

   Ⓑ discourage skaters   Ⓓ break down

On the lines below, write your own question based on "Designing a Skatepark." Circle the correct picture on the left to show the level of the question you wrote.

_____

_____

_____

_____

___

On a separate piece of paper . . .

• Write a sentence that uses the word *liability*.

• What features would you include in a skatepark in your local area? Consider the age and interests of your target population in your reasons and evidence.

___

Answer Key

Accept appropriate responses for the final three entries on the question-and-answer pages.

Racing into History (page 11)
1. A   3. A
2. B   4. D

An Oddly Delicious Fruit (page 13)
1. D   3. D
2. C   4. C

A Thrilling Ride (page 15)
1. C   3. D
2. B   4. C

The Sleep Hormone (page 17)
1. A   3. D
2. B   4. B

The World's Wildest Weather (page 19)
1. D   3. C
2. A   4. C

A Code for Health (page 21)
1. C   3. D
2. C   4. B

Folly or Investment? (page 23)
1. C   3. B
2. A   4. A

War on the Home Front (page 25)
1. C   3. A
2. A   4. B

Our Valuable Money (page 27)
1. B   3. B
2. A   4. C

Vending Machines (page 29)
1. B   3. D
2. C   4. A

The History of Fashion (page 31)
1. B   3. A
2. C   4. D

René Descartes (page 33)
1. B   3. D
2. A   4. A

César Chávez (page 35)
1. C   3. D
2. A   4. B

J.R.R. Tolkien (page 37)
1. A   3. D
2. C   4. B

Admiral Hopper (page 39)
1. D   3. A
2. C   4. B

Ultimate: The Game (page 41)
1. B   3. B
2. A   4. D

The Nobel Prizes (page 43)
1. C   3. B
2. A   4. B

Giving a Great Speech (page 45)
1. D   3. B
2. C   4. A

Designing a Skatepark (page 47)
1. B   3. A
2. B   4. D